BASKETBALL KING
THE JEREMY WHITHAM STORY

By Rebecca Ballew Dockum

ISBN 979-8-9881331-0-0

Cover Graphic Artist by Alysha Coy Desharnais.

Photographs provided by Jeremy Whitham.

Photo Editor Kyle Dockum

All logos and names are used with written permission.

Little
Branch

PUBLISHING

$14.99
ISBN 979-8-9881331-0-0
51499>

9 798988 133100

BASKETBALL KING

THE JEREMY WHITHAM STORY

By Rebecca Ballew Dockum

Baby Jeremy was born ....

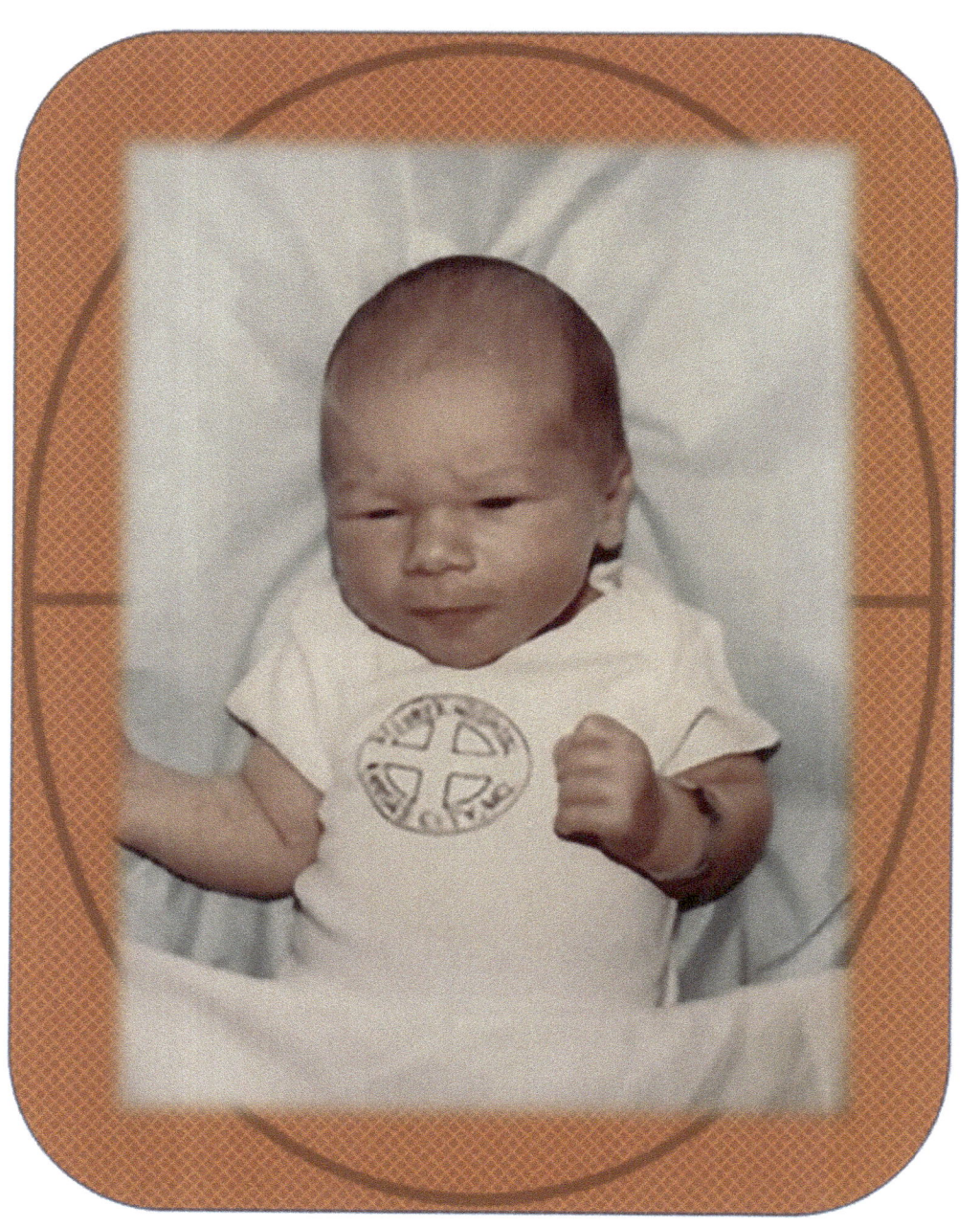

Baby Jeremy was born with special needs.

He doesn't cuddle.

He doesn't want to be touched.

Jeremy likes to be alone.

Jeremy reaches for balloons in the store.

He wants to take all of them home, but his Mother says, "Just one."

He likes how it floats on a string.

Jeremy loves balloons.

Jeremy spins things: wheels, propellers, and merry-go-rounds.

Around and around, he spins, saying, "Nana-nana."

He uses sign language to tell others what he needs.

The only thing he loves more than spinning is his balloons.

Four-year-old Jeremy goes to the Judevine® Center.

He traces the lines between the white wall tiles.

At the center, he finds his voice.

Jeremy loves to talk about balloons.

Jeremy's grandmother gives him a basketball.

It holds air like a balloon.

He traces the black lines that run around the ball.

He takes his basketball everywhere.

Name Jeremy

THE FIRST THANKSGIVING DAY

Directions: Read each sentence. Write a word on each blank to complete each sentence. Illustrate part of this story in the space below.

1. The Indians and the Pilgrims went hunting in the woods for a _food_.

2. The Indians taught the Pilgrims how to grow _CORN_.

3. They prepared a big feast of _noodles and Kit Kats_.

4. They were thankful for _noodles, Kit Kat, basketballs and balloons_

At school, the teacher helps Jeremy write about the first Thanksgiving.

His teacher asks him to make a report on how something is made.

He mails a letter to the *Voit* corporation and asks about how they make basketballs.

It is a surprise when they send him a case of balls.

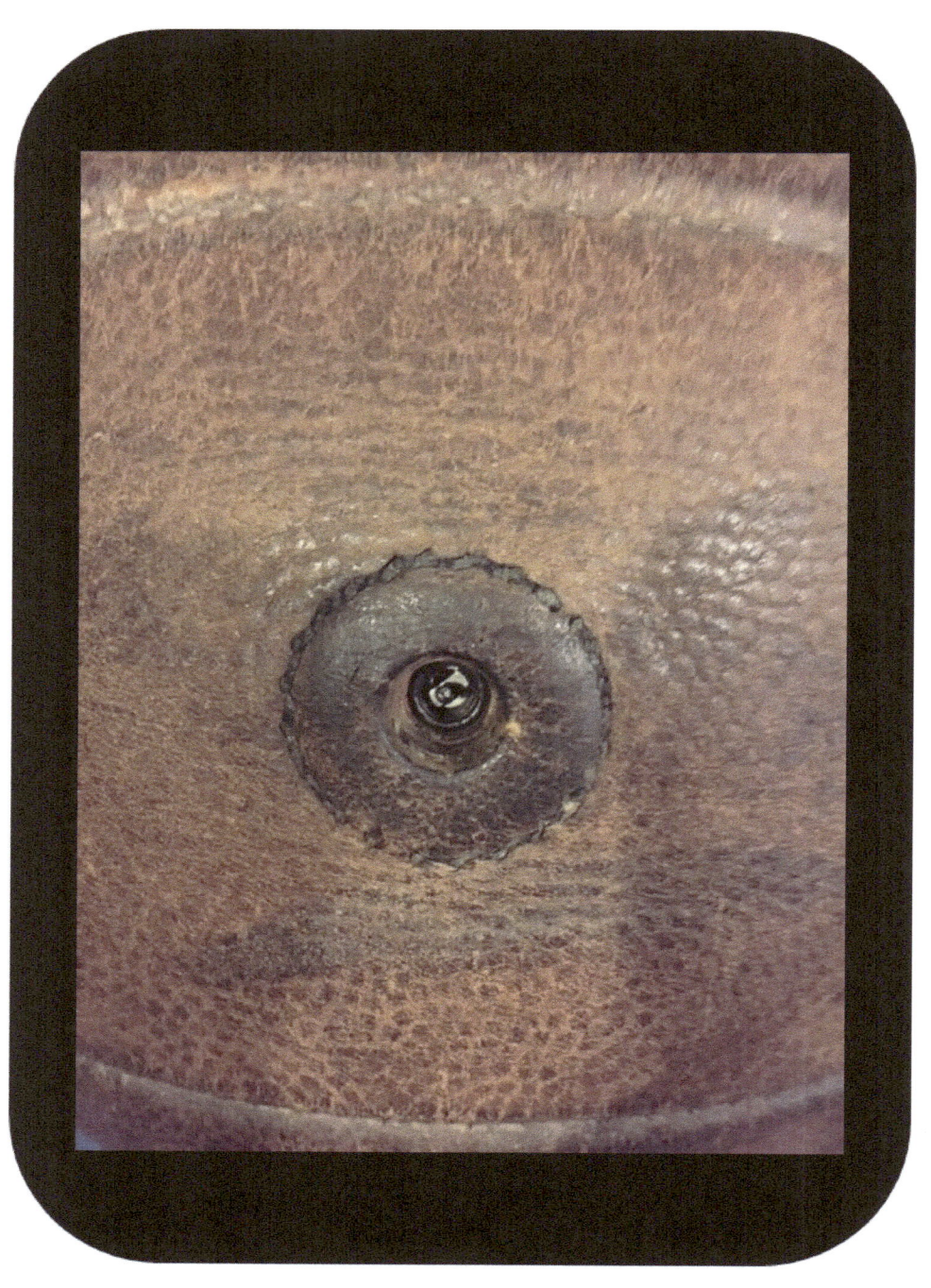

Now, Jeremy can fix flat basketballs.

Basketballs have a rubber bladder inside to hold air.

This ball looks like it has a belly button.

The valve is where you inflate the bladder.

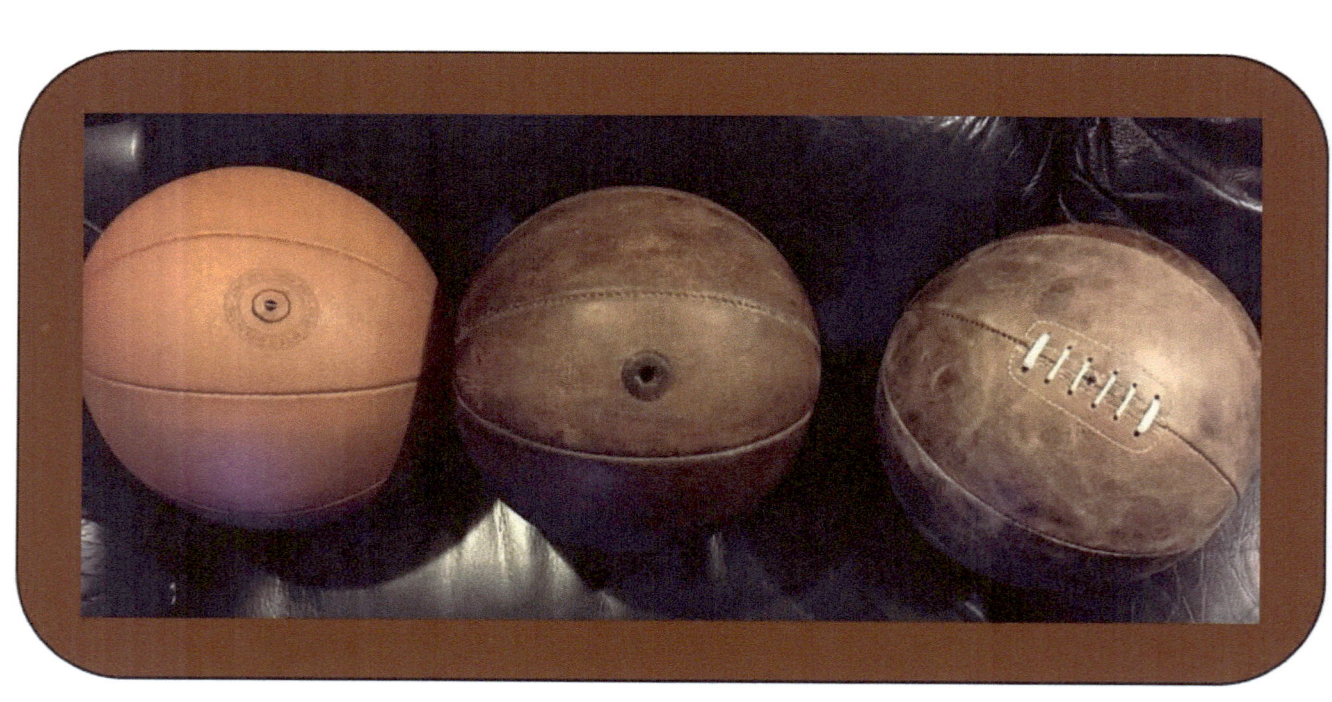

Today, Jeremy has old and new basketballs.

The oldest is leather and is laced closed.

Now they make them from molded rubber or synthetic materials.

Can you tell which ball is the oldest?

Jeremy says basketballs help him.

He never feels lonely if he has one with him.

They give him something to talk about.

He looks for basketballs everywhere he goes.

People give Jeremy basketballs.

His room is full of balls.

His mother says, "You must get rid of some of these."

He gives a few to children who need toys.

Jeremy likes to talk to his friends about basketballs.

Collectors from all over the world send him emails.

He loves to show his collection on the news.

One reporter even gave him a football from the Super Bowl.

Jeremy says basketballs have helped him.

They give him courage to do things.

Jeremy learned to drive so he can find more basketballs.

He loves a good challenge.

Jeremy still gives basketballs to children.

He thinks everybody needs one.

He thinks having a basketball could give you courage.

Courage can help you find new things you like to do.

Jeremy has over 1,000 basketballs.

He has one of the largest collections in the United States.

You can visit his museum in Missouri.

Jeremy wants to know: *How many basketballs do you have?*

Meet Jeremy Whitham

Jeremy has one of the largest collections in the United States. He displays over 1,000 unique basketballs in Osceola, Missouri. His collection includes a ball from the debut of Olympic basketball in 1936.

People around the world are inspired to help him build up the museum.

Jeremy, born in 1984, developed seizures from low blood sugar. He underwent surgery to remove 95% of his pancreas. By age two, his height, weight, and physical strength caused doctors to believe he had a form of giantism.

While attending the Judevine® Center for Autism in Saint Louis, Missouri, Jeremy learned social skills and Signing Exact English through the center's competency-based training. At age four, he started speaking in full sentences with his first being, "I want chocolate."

Jeremy with his kidney donor Pastor Jack Coultas.

In 2017, Jeremy received a kidney transplant. During recovery, he made plans for his museum where others can enjoy his collection and talk with him about basketballs.

Judevine® Center for Autism

Judevine® Center for Autism, located in Saint Louis, Missouri, gives support to individuals with autism and their families.

www.judevine.org

Signing Exact English (SEE) matches signs with the English Language and allows individuals to learn standard English like hearing individuals.

www.signingexactenglish.com

McPherson Globe Refiners, the 1933 amateur team from McPherson, Kansas, joined the first 1936 United States Olympic Basketball Team and won the gold medal. Their nickname became *The Tallest Team in the World*.

www.visitmcpherson.com

Contact Jeremy Whitham at Jeremy_Whitham@hotmail.com.

Rebecca Ballew Dockum began storytelling as a child, deep in the wooded Missouri Ozarks. Who wouldn't develop an imagination with nearby towns named Tightwad and Toad Suck?

She believes anyone can accomplish their life goals despite disabilities. Rebecca lives in Phoenix, Arizona where she encourages others to write their own tales.

www.ingramcontent.com/pod-product-compliance
Lightning Source LLC
Chambersburg PA
CBHW041522120626
46551CB00018B/2543